Caregiver Storm

Make More Money and Build Customer Loyalty by Guiding Clients through the Elder Care Process

Ten Guiding Principles to share with your clients
so they can survive the "Caregiver Storm"
when elderly loved ones require help and planning
for complicated legal and financial needs.

Ben A. Neiburger, JD, CPA

Table of Contents

A Love Story

Let's start with a love story.

About 10 years ago, a family came to me asking for Medicaid planning advice. Medicaid planning is an estate planning and public benefits planning technique that can reduce long-term health care costs. This technique uses the Medicaid program to pay all or a portion of a person's long-term care benefits, instead of completely exhausting assets.

Mike shuffled in with his son Jason one sunny morning with his head hung low and a look of utter exhaustion and frustration on his face. Jason was holding on to his elbow. As they sat down, I asked Mike what was wrong and he looked at me.

"My love, Laura, she hallucinates," he said.

"As I drive down the road she claims to see her mother and grandmother on the corner, and I tell her they're not there. Then she yells at me saying they are, and one minute later, at the next intersection, the same thing happens again. It's driving me crazy. The doctor says she has Alzheimer's disease."

Mike slammed his fist on the table in frustration and said, "I'm not going to put Laura in a nursing home."

Then, Jason looked at me and shook his head. His father looked down at something on my desk, distracted.

"Mike, how's your heart?" I asked.

"Oh it's bad. I'm on medications and I feel so stressed," Mike responded.

"Okay, how high is your stress level?"

"My stress level is terrible. Laura wakes me up three or four times a night. I'm afraid she's going to wander on the street, so I have to get up and make sure she doesn't go downstairs. Whenever I hear a noise, I get up to make sure the door is locked so she doesn't go outside. It's driving me crazy."

"Then you're not sleeping well?" I responded.

"No, my sleep is terrible," Mike said.

"Mike, are you aware of what caregiver stress is?"

He responded, "Yes, I have lots of stress."

"Mike, did you know the statistics say the healthy spouse dies before the ill spouse almost one third of the time?"

Then Mike looked up, his eyes opened wide by surprise, and he asked, "Really?"

"Yes," I responded. Let me ask you, how well can you take care of Laura when you're dead?"

Dead silence. A look of shock overcame him.

"Mike, I'm sure your children will do a fine job taking care of Laura, but nobody knows her as well as you do— nobody can care for her as well as you can," I explained. "There is no better advocate for her happiness and safety than you. So it's your job to take care of you first. Once you are set, then you can make sure she gets the best care.

To do this, you need to change your role from being her primary caregiver to being her caregiving advocate. Her caregiving advocate will make sure she gets the best care there is."

I explained to Mike, that because of his caregiver stress, he needed to put Laura in a nursing home so he could keep himself healthy and make sure she received the best care.

"I know you'll visit her almost every day and I know you'll be looking over her," I said. "Remember, since her short-term memory only lasts a minute, she isn't going to remember if you're there or not. She isn't going to remember if you visited or if you didn't visit. If she gets mad at you for not being there, she will forget she is mad a minute later. So, you can visit periodically. You can make sure the staff is treating her right. You can take the time you need to keep yourself healthy, to visit your friends, to spend time with your children and grandchildren."

Mike placed Laura in a nursing home within two weeks. The home was in a plain looking brick building, nothing fancy, but it was clean, the staff was friendly, and there were always fresh flowers. We were able to use some Medicaid planning techniques to exclude Mike's IRA, car and the family home from Medicaid's spousal asset rules. This means that those assets did not count against Mike or Laura for Laura's Medicaid eligibility. Accordingly, Laura immediately became eligible for Medicaid benefits to pay for her room and board at the nursing home.

Two months after Mike admitted Laura to the nursing home, the Illinois Department of Human Services, Illinois' Medicaid agency, sent Mike the letter approving

Laura's Medicaid. I called Mike, and he came into my office to see the approval letter. After he read it and I explained what it meant, Mike looked at me and smiled. It was as if the greatest weight in the world was just lifted off his shoulders.

When Mike and Laura's children were growing up, Mike worked and Laura kept the house and raised the kids. He worked as a printer for a commercial publisher and put in long hours when his kids were young. As a result, Mike wasn't as close to his children as he wanted to be. In addition, once he retired, Mike was caring for Laura and unable to spend the time he wanted with his children and grandchildren. After he put Laura in the nursing home, Mike found that he could rest and focus on himself and the rest of his family. He started playing golf again with his buddies and he started spending time with his family. He would go to birthday parties. He would babysit. He would take the grandchildren out. Mike reconnected with his family. This was the lull before the storm.

Two years had passed when Mike called me and asked, "Ben, do you remember that estate planning you prepared for me when we did the Medicaid planning for Laura?"

"Yes Mike, I remember that."

"I want to know if all my affairs are in order."

"I think they are."

"Well, I want to be sure. I saw a doctor recently because I was experiencing a lot of cramping in my hands and feet and some muscle weakness. They ran a number of tests, and I just got the results. I have ALS."

ALS is a disease that leaves the mind alone while gradually degenerating the neurons in the brain that affect muscle movement. With ALS, most of the person's motor neurons degenerate and die. ALS is inevitably fatal, as it eventually leaves the sufferer unable to move and breathe. There are drugs designed to slow this process down, but the disease will run its course.

While planning for Laura, Mike not only became educated in which public benefit options were available to his family, he also did some special planning for himself. Statistics show that the mortality risk for a caregiver spouse is 62% higher than for a non-caregiving spouse. So Mike completed a special estate plan that would disinherit his spouse if he died first, since any money Laura would inherit would need to be spent on her care. Under his estate plan, if he died first, the children would have the use of his money to support their mother and buy her things Medicaid wouldn't pay for. Mike had his estate plan designed to accommodate any disability he might develop, so didn't have to make any changes to his estate plan after his diagnosis.

During the planning process for Laura, Mike unknowingly applied many of the elder care principles this booklet covers. He hired professionals to teach him what he needed to know to make the most appropriate decisions for his family. He planned ahead. He took time for himself. Because he was proactive and we sheltered his income and assets from Laura's long-term care costs, Mike was able to maintain his dignity and independence as the disease gradually worsened. Because of the work we did protecting his assets and income from the costs of Laura's long-term care, he hired a caregiver to live with him in his house to help him with the tasks he couldn't do himself. He had enough money so that he didn't have to rely on his children. His children did not have to put their lives on hold to care for him. Instead, Mike's children could check on him and his caregiver and make sure he was getting good care. They could spend quality time visiting him since they were not the primary caregivers. Because there was no caregiver stress for the children, the siblings' relationships remained strong and the family stayed close.

Mike went on like this for another year. He still went to family birthday parties, although he couldn't babysit as much. His caregiver carted him around to all the places he wanted to go. Then, on a sunny fall day when the leaves from the trees began to fall, Mike called me again. His frail voice asked, "Ben, are all my affairs in order?"

"Mike, if you did everything I told you to do it should all be fine," I responded.

"Okay, I think I did. Thank you for all you have done. Goodbye."

That was the last conversation I had with Mike. He died several weeks later.

Six months later at a local Chamber of Commerce meeting, I saw Mike's son Jason. Jason came up to me saying, "Ben, did you hear how dad died?"

"No," I said. "I didn't hear how your father died. Can you tell me?"

"Yes. Right before he died, he told all us kids that he wanted momma to come home and visit him.

At this point he hadn't gotten up very often, he hadn't gotten dressed to go out in weeks, and he hadn't shaved and done other personal grooming. But for this visit, he had his caregiver get him up, put on his favorite yellow Izod polo, shave him and sit him in his favorite chair in the living room.

We brought momma home and sat her in the chair next to dad. My sisters and all of our kids were there. Mom and dad were holding hands the whole time. Even though mom didn't seem to know who anyone was, she was very happy and chatted with an imaginary person in babble-speak non-stop. The grandchildren talked to both of them: dad answered silly questions and the children giggled at mom's responses to their questions. My father had a big, but tired smile on his face. It was a happy moment.

After an hour and a half of this, dad turned his head using his headrest for support. He was very weak.

"Laura, my love, I am very tired," he said. "I am going to go to sleep now." And then daddy died holding hands with his wife, in the presence of his children and grandchildren."

~

This is a scene of a family facing terrible illnesses, which took two loved ones before their time. But the family had as much closure and harmony as there could be in a situation like that. It's the way the end should and can be.

Many end-of-life diseases are incurable or won't improve. However, if you know what to look out for and how to find resources, you can get through the process in the best way possible.

This is essential since you don't really have a choice about the situation you're in. Use the elder care principles to become more educated and prepared for the inevitable, so that your family can live on with their dignity intact.

This book will provide financial professionals with the legal and relational know-how to share these principles with clients to help them and their family members survive this journey. Of course, when you help the family get through one of the most difficult times of their lives, you become a central trusted figure within that family. And once you have this level of trust, more client referrals, assets under management, and letters of engagement will naturally follow.

Legal and financial professionals can be the ones to hold the umbrella and guide toward "Brighter Skies" during the silver tsunami of Baby Boomers bringing a "Caregiver Storm" upon clients and their families.

Effectively Guiding Your Clients

How do you help? How do you make a difference? How do you guide your clients through this difficult process?

The starting point should be the annual review you have with your clients. The first thing that you should ask them, after pleasantries and the main financial planning business concludes, is how their parents are doing. You'll be surprised at the responses you'll receive because there will always be something going on with a parent, no matter how rich or poor they are, no matter their location or sophistication. The adult children will most likely act as the caregivers. However, your clients will look to you, as their advisor, to guide them through the process. They want you to educate them about what they don't know, and where they can go to get the information, knowledge, and referrals they need to take care of their parents. Your clients want to ensure they maintain their dignity, sanity, and their own lives. This is what the Ten Guiding Principles are for.

Caring for a loved one who needs a lot of support, or who is suffering from dementia, is some of the hardest work any of your clients will ever have to do in their lives, both physically and emotionally. These Ten Guiding Principles will help you guide your clients through the caregiving process and ensure that they can provide the best care possible for their loved ones, so that your clients can help their loved ones maintain their dignity and wishes at the end of their lives.

By helping clients understand and implement these Ten Guiding Principles, you will help them keep their health, life, career, marriage, and family intact.

1. Put No One Else Before You and Your Family
2. Let Others Help You
3. Act Only With Legal Authority
4. Rest. You are only human.
5. Honor Your Loved One and Preserve Their Independence as Long as Medically Advisable
6. Make a Financial Plan
7. Respect Your Loved One's End-of-Life Wishes.
8. You Can't Control a Progressive Disease or Sudden Illness
9. A Nursing Home Placement Isn't a Death Sentence
10. Try to Mitigate Family Conflict

As we explain each of these topics in the following pages, the tone is as if speaking directly to clients. Please share these pages and the checklists with them. They will become a valuable guide that will help you, help them prepare for and get through the elder care process.

Guiding Principle One
Put No One Else Before You and Your Family

You have a moral obligation to care for your parents, spouse and children. To do this well, you need to be informed, plan ahead, and take care of yourself first. The earlier the better.

In our love story, the family asked for advice early enough in the disease process where they were able to do some planning. The family's only real mistake was not catching the caregiver stress earlier. They did avoid that tragedy, however. Learning about Laura's Alzheimer's disease was a panic-free process, and they were able to take care of her until the absolute end.

Mike created an estate plan to avoid the probate process making after-death asset transitions easier. Because of the planning, they had a chance to enjoy their lives a little more, despite the diseases, and ensured they received care and a chance for all family members to gain closure. Even with all that happened to them, this it was still extremely difficult. They did the right thing by putting the healthy family members first so those healthy family members could care for the sick ones more effectively. As a result, they were able to ensure Laura had better care. This is what this Guiding Principle is about.

Families should:

Become informed. Most people haven't gone through the elder care process before. There are a lot of moving parts in providing elder care, so the more you know about your elder's health, doctors, treatment options, living situation, and legal and financial life, the better you'll be able to make the right choices for your loved one.

Plan ahead. While it's always nice to plan ahead, it is not always possible if you have your children and parents to look after. However, you have the ability to plan ahead—even for emergencies. You'll need to decide where your loved one will live both short term and long term, what medical and everyday care they will need in order to be independent, get their legal documents in order so you can speak for them without going to court, and accommodate any special family dynamics you have.

Take care of themselves first. Elder care requires an incredible amount of work. If you don't pay attention to yourself, the strain you experience will decrease both your effectiveness and your ability to make wise decisions. In addition, because of this strain, you won't even know it. If you're not both physically and mentally healthy, you won't be able to provide your loved one with the care they deserve.

Guiding Principle One – Check Lists

Become Informed

Learn the lay of the land. Depending on needs, you should learn about:

❏ Your loved one's caregiving needs and the options

❏ General medical practitioners with extensive geriatric experience in your loved one's area

❏ Options on where to live (at home, independent living, assisted living, memory care, skilled nursing)

❏ Find an elder law attorney to educate you and your family about the choices you will need to make in planning for long-term care, disability and avoiding Probate and to help with the documentation necessary to put your choices into practice.

❏ If appropriate, find a financial planner to help you create a stronger stream of income from your investments and retirement accounts

❏ Find an accountant to help you find additional income tax deductions (including those that give you credit for medical expenses and long-term care expenses) so you have more money left over to use to produce a stream of income.

Plan Ahead

❑ Living Arrangements – Know when to stay in the home and when to move to another place. You do not need to have a place picked out unless placement is imminent (facilities change frequently—but knowing the types of places that are available will be helpful in reducing stress later).

❑ Medical care – Be able to speak with your loved one's medical doctor and have your loved one sign HIPAA information release forms so that you can get access to their private medical information when you need it, and so that you understand the everyday care and medications your loved one needs.

❑ Legal documents – Without powers of attorney for property/finance, you will have no access to your loved one's money to pay bills and expenses. Without healthcare powers of attorney, or other medical advanced directives, you will have no access to your loved one's medical records or be able to direct medical professionals in your loved one's care, especially in cases in which they cannot direct the care themselves.

❑ Family Dynamics – If you have a dysfunctional family unit, get some help and set up your legal documents so that the appropriate family member (or independent professional/trustee) has the power of manage finances and health. If you think there may be a family fight or abuse, find a way to mediate problems ahead of time, or just hunker down and wait for the storm.

Take Care of Yourself First

This is going to be rough. If you cannot take care of yourself, you will not be an effective caregiver.

❑ Seek help from professionals including getting a geriatric assessment of your loved one. (see Guiding Principle Two) This will provide a "map" of what you need to do.

❑ Try to get help from everyone else too (friends, family, neighbors) – these checklists make it easy to let folks know what needs to get done

❑ Don't not try to do the impossible

❑ Watch your physical health

❑ Get adequate sleep

❑ Do not give up your life to provide caregiving

❑ Get a therapist or counselor to help you manage stress and guilt

Most people haven't gone through the elder care process before. There are a lot of moving parts in providing elder care, so the more you know about your elder's health, doctors, treatment options, living situation, and legal and financial life, the better you'll be able to make the right choices for your loved one.

Guiding Principle Two
Let Others Help You

By letting others help you, you'll be better able to help your loved one.

Find a trusted team of experts to help you through the health, legal and financial issues associated with end-of-life healthcare and planning. Geriatricians, care managers, elder law attorneys, accountants and financial planners can all help.

In our love story, somewhat late in the process, the family hired a lawyer to educate them about the issues they were facing. They also had a financial planner involved to plan income streams from Mike's assets and retirement monies so Mike could live on his own and not be impoverished by Laura's sickness. Later, as Mike's own disease progressed, not only did they have a professional help with the caregiving, but they also involved teams of doctors to manage the disease process, which allowed Mike to be as independent as long as possible and to maintain his dignity. The family could not have done this without outside help from a team of experts.

As the number and severity of a person's disabilities increase, so does the complexity of the care. "Care" in this sense means not only attending to a person's daily needs and healthcare, but to their finances and legal affairs. Each one of the areas of expertise we list below is complex, and a person cannot deal with all of them alone. As the caregiver, you will need to hire these professionals on to help educate you about the issues you may face. Some of the professionals you may need to see only once or twice (elder law attorneys, accountants, and financial planners), and for others (such as geriatricians and care managers), it will be a continual, long-term relationship.

In addition, many caregivers try taking the entire responsibility for looking after a sick individual. When they can't do this (because it's humanly impossible) they feel guilty and the quality of care decreases. Many times, they fail to realize they've bitten off more than they can chew. And if you don't ask for help, you won't receive any. As a caregiver, you must communicate to your team because you cannot assume that they know what you need. You may be putting up a good front leading everyone around you to think you have everything under control. So speak out and find a team of people who can help you.

Geriatricians

One of the keys to successful elder care is getting a geriatrician. A geriatrician is a primary care physician who focuses their practice on the elderly. The elderly react differently to trauma, drugs, and treatment than younger people. The extra training geriatricians receive, and the care they provide, can keep your loved one as healthy as possible. Geriatricians can help coordinate care, especially when more than three medical specialists are involved. Because of their narrow focus, medical specialists do not focus on the rest of the body as a whole. So, when you have several specialists treating several different conditions on an elderly body, someone with extensive medical knowledge of the older body must be there to coordinate the care (including specialist's advice), manage side effects of various medications, and make sure that each specialist is aware of the things the other specialists are doing while coordinating what each does.

Obtaining a geriatrician is increasingly difficult in our current "pay for service system" where doctors are paid by the procedures they perform and not by the people they take care of. The decreasing reimbursements through Medicare is causing a problem and reducing the number of physicians that go into this specialty. You'll be able to get services under Medicare—you just won't be able to get a doctor. So, for now, finding a dedicated geriatrician is the best thing that you can do.

Care Managers

Care managers are nurses and social workers with private practices that provide high-level care for elders and others with disabilities. If you don't live in the same area as your elder, or you lead a busy life, hiring a care manager can help you care for your loved one. A care manager can also quickly educate you on what you need to know about your elder's living and health-care options.

While care managers are there to help, you may become overwhelmed by all the advice and guidance you're receiving. The biggest question people caregiving for their parents ask me is, "What do we do? The nursing home says this, and the hospital says that, and the really nice social worker says we need to leave the hospital in two hours because Medicare payments are running out. We don't know what to do, and we read this blog on the Internet …" et cetera.

In addition to concerns about how to appropriately deal with aging loved ones, it seems everything connected with dying and getting old is expensive. Care managers are meant to help guide the adult children and healthy spouse through the process. They'll help you assess your concerns and to guide the family. Geriatric care managers act as sons and daughters on the ground to manage mom and dad. If your parents go to the hospital and you are out of town, you'll have a person who works independent of the hospital tell you the state of your parents' health, so you know whether or not you need to make a trip to see them. Using geriatric care managers is a fantastic way to help you manage health care as well as the logistical aspects of caregiving. They also do a good job of teaching you what you really need to worry about, and when you need outside advocacy.

Elder Law Attorneys

Elder Law attorneys are attorneys with specialized knowledge who can guide you through the byzantine labyrinth of laws that surround an elder's medical and financial decisions, health-care advocacy, and finding sources of money to pay for long-term care. Advice from an elder law attorney is well worth the cost. It can save hundreds of thousands of dollars.

If you are seeing an estate planning attorney instead, make sure that attorney has a deep knowledge of elder law issues.

Important Elder Law issues include:

- ✓ Estates and Trusts

- ✓ Powers of Attorney

- ✓ Guardianships/Conservatorships

- ✓ Social Security

- ✓ Medicare

- ✓ Medicaid,

- ✓ Housing

- ✓ Disability Advocacy

- ✓ Assisted Living and Nursing Home Advocacy

- ✓ Experience managing difficult family situations

An attorney with just an estate planning background isn't going to know everything necessary to help you. Be wary of the estate planner who insists they can do everything and know everything because that might not be the case.

Financial Planners and Accountants

Financial planners and accountants are necessary to maximize your elder's income and keep his or her taxes as low as possible so there's enough money to pay for his or her care and lodging.

Although many people focus on trying to get Medicaid to pay for care, the real solution is to do everything you can to avoid using public benefits such as Medicaid for supporting long-term care expenses. To do this, your family must take advantage of income tax deductions for long-term care and other medical expenses. If a person must take monies from IRAs or retirement accounts, an accountant can help minimize the income taxes that those withdrawals create.

Financial planners can help you squeeze extra income out of investible assets. If your loved one has enough assets, he or she might be able to generate enough income from those assets with the help of a financial planner. This income (along with social security and any pension income) can pay for long-term care costs without touching principle. Of course, generating income of $6,000 to $8,000—the cost for long-term care in Northern Illinois— per month might be difficult for some families. If so, there are other planning options that an elder law attorney can help you implement to use Medicaid to pay for care at some point in the future.

Guiding Principle Two - Checklist

❑ Let others help you, don't do it all yourself. (Sharing the Checklists in this book is one easy way to ask!)

❑ Find a geriatrician or internist with geriatric experience to manage overall medical healthcare; especially if more than three doctors are involved.

❑ Make sure your elder has regular dentist visits.

❑ Find a care manager to help with the difficult things and coordinating services, if needed.

❑ Find caregivers (either full time or part time) to help take the pressure off the family caregiver.

❑ Find an elder law attorney to teach you the issues you should pay attention to and know about. They can also help you with documents and other legal tools so you can manage your loved ones legal and financial affairs.

❑ Find a financial planner to help your loved one to maximize income.

❑ Find an accountant to help reduce taxes and find deductions for care expenses and nursing homes.

❑ Investigate community-based programs for additional help (such as home-delivered meals, social outlets, adult day care services, respite care, emergency response devices, etc.)

❑ Involve Clergy and your elder's religious community.

Guiding Principle Three
Act Only With Legal Authority

Make sure there is an estate plan in place. At minimum, a person's estate plan should include financial and health care powers of attorney along with a will (and sometimes a trust).

In our love story, Mike was able to create an estate plan that sheltered most of his estate from his wife's long-term care costs. In fact, he was in the not-so-small percentage of people who do not survive the sick spouse. Without this plan, his family could not have made appropriate decisions for Mike during his own slow decline from ALS without the courts being involved. Because they did do the planning, they were able to protect his dignity and allow him to be independent, almost until the very end. In addition, our planning saved almost all of his assets from long-term care costs.

Powers of Attorney

There will come a time where you may need to make health care and financial decisions for your loved one when she cannot make decisions for herself. Remember that when making decisions for her, you are, in a sense, stepping into her shoes and acting as you think she would act. This means that, when making these decisions, you must substitute her wishes for yours.

The law will not allow you to make decisions for a person who is not mentally competent unless that person signed written documentation (called powers of attorney or, sometimes, advanced directives) that authorizes you to make decisions for them. A person can't sign these documents if they don't have the mental capacity to understand what they mean.

A person has mental capacity to sign a power of attorney if her mind can understand:

- ✓ what it will mean for her if she signs the power of attorney
- ✓ what the power of attorney says
- ✓ what a power of attorney is, and
- ✓ the legal effect to her when she signs the power of attorney

If you do not have powers of attorney for someone, then a judge must grant permission to make decisions for that person. That court procedure, called a guardianship, is very expensive ($5,000 to $10,000 or more). In some states, the financial portion of the guardianship is called a conservatorship while the person portion is called the "guardianship." In other states, you have a guardian for the "person" (health decisions) and a guardian of the "estate" (financial decisions and management).

Protect your loved one's dignity and privacy by having her sign a financial and a health care power of attorney before it's too late. If she needs to use Medicaid to help pay her long-term care expenses, put in place a robust financial power of attorney. This power of attorney should permit the power of attorney agent (the person who is acting for the elder) to use Medicaid planning techniques including the ability to gift assets including a home to a "caretaker" child, creating and funding special trusts, and to modify an estate plan. While these types of powers of attorney are very specialized and have advantages, they come along with disadvantages too. We highly recommend that you hire an elder law attorney to create them and advise you on how to use them.

A health-care power of attorney gives you access to your loved one's private health care information and allows you to make health care and placement decisions for him or her.

In most cases (other than when families are fighting or there is financial elder abuse), you will not need a guardianship if you have proper powers of attorney in place. Of course, a person can only sign powers of attorney documents when they are mentally competent and can still understand what they are signing.

Health Care Privacy Consents

The Health Insurance Portability and Accountability Act (HIPAA) requires medical providers to protect certain health care information. HIPAA prohibits them from disclosing that information to people other than their patients unless the patient signs a consent permitting them to disclose that information. These consents are called HIPAA consents. The HIPAA rules impose large fines on providers who do not follow the rules. HIPAA rules do permit providers to disclose information to a patient's personal representative (usually, the person the patient appoints as his health care power of attorney) or to the persons listed on a disclosure consent form that the patient signs.

Wills

A will provides instruction for the distribution of property you own when you die in any manner you choose (subject to the forced heirship laws of some states, like Illinois, that prevent disinheriting a spouse using a will). Your will cannot, however, govern the distribution of property that passes outside of your probate estate, such as certain joint property, life insurance, retirement plans, and employee death benefits, unless the property is payable to your estate (or your estate is the beneficiary of the property).

Wills can have various degrees of complexity and can help you achieve a wide range of family and estate tax objectives. In general, a "simple will" provides for the outright distribution of assets, a "testamentary trust will" establishes one or more trusts upon your death, a "pour over will" leaves some probate assets to a trust you create during your lifetime. In most cases, the purpose of a trust is to ensure continued property management and creditor protection for the surviving family members, to provide for charities, and to minimize taxes.

In addition to distributing your assets to your spouse, children, etc., your will may accomplish other important objectives including:

✓ You designate a guardian for your minor child or children. By judicious use of a trust and appointment of a trustee, you can eliminate the need for bonds and supervision by the Court regarding the care of each child's estate.

✓ You designate an executor of your estate in your will.

28

✓ You may choose to acknowledge or otherwise provide for a child (e.g., stepchild, godchild, etc.), an elderly parent, or other individuals in whom you have an interest.

✓ If you are acting as custodian for the assets of a child or grandchild under the Uniform Gift (or Transfers) to Minors Act, you may designate your successor custodian and avoid the expense and hassle of a court appointment.

Good planning through gifting in your will can also enhance your support of religious, educational, and other charitable causes.

Trusts

A trust is a legal device that acts as a "container" that holds money and property. You can think of a trust like a bowl that holds candy where the bowl represents the trust and the candy represents your money and property. The person who holds their bowls is called the trustee. The trust contains instructions on how the trustee can use the Trust's assets.

During his or her lifetime, a person can create a trust called a living trust (also known as a revocable trust) that:

✓ You create during your lifetime,

✓ You can change whenever you wish

✓ Has a trustee, and

✓ Owns property that (generally) you have transferred to it during your life.

Generally, assets that a living trust owns do not go through the probate process and are not available to the public's prying eyes. Much has been written recently regarding the use of living trusts as a solution for a wide variety of problems associated with estate planning through wills. Some attorneys regularly recommend the use of such trusts, while others believe their value has been somewhat overstated. You should choose to use a living trust after you consider a number of factors.

While you are living, the trustee (who may be you) is generally responsible for managing the property as you direct for your benefit. Upon your death, the trustee is generally directed to either distribute the trust property to your beneficiaries, or to continue to hold and manage it for the long-term benefit of your beneficiaries. Like a will, a living trust can provide for the distribution of property upon your death. However, unlike a will, it can provide a way to manage your property during your life, and authorize the trustee to manage the property and use it for your benefit (and your family's) if you should become incapacitated. This will help avoid the hassle of a court process to appoint a guardian for that purpose.

Generally, trusts that you set up yourself cannot protect your assets against your own creditors, but they can protect an inheritance that someone receives from you from their own creditors. In addition, sometimes trusts are used in Medicaid planning to protect assets if the spouse who lives in the community dies before the spouse living in the nursing home.

Insurance and Loss

Insurance protects against catastrophe. Without insurance, a loss can destroy economic survival for the entire family. You should take an in-depth look at your loved one's insurance coverage and update your review with your loved one's insurance agent on a yearly basis. Get copies of each insurance policy and make sure it is current and in force. Insurance coverage to consider include:

✓ Homeowners insurance (covers possessions destroyed by fire and water, provides monies for temporary living arrangements and to rebuild)

✓ Automobile insurance

✓ Valuables insurance (jewelry, antiques, etc.)

✓ Life insurance

✓ Disability insurance for caregivers who also work

✓ Health insurance, including Medicare and the supplemental insurance that covers Medicare's co-pay and cost sharing provisions

In addition, to recover monies from insurance if there is a loss, you must be able to prove that you had the items in the first place. Always video or take picture of the contents of your loved one's house including any valuables they may have.

Guiding Principle Three - Checklist

❑ Make plans to review and update (or, if there are none, create) all legal documents

❑ Power of Attorney for Health Care/Advanced Medical Directive (helps you make health care and medical decisions for another while they live)

❑ Power of Attorney for Property/Finance (helps you make financial decisions for another while they live)

❑ Trust (helps make financial decisions for a person's assets that the trust holds/avoids probate after death on those assets and directs who inherits those assets)

❑ Will (instructions for who inherits following death)

❑ Health care information privacy consent (HIPAA consent – in addition to the health care power of attorney, it helps get access to health care info)

❑ Make sure key family members have copies of documents and understand how they work (or they know who to call for an explanation)

❑ Check Health Insurance coverage (Medicare and supplemental Medicare insurance)

❑ Check for Non-Health Insurance Coverage (life insurance, homeowner, insurance for specific valuables, auto, disability, long term care)

❑ Take pictures or videos of possessions in case of insurance covered loss, theft, or estate dispute.

Guiding Principle Four
Rest. You are only human.

Make sure you rest, regularly take time off, and get help. As the caregiving process begins, you will want to give your loved one the best care humanly possible. Many times, this requires an incredible amount of time, effort, blood, sweat, and tears. Even the strongest of us will only last a matter of weeks or months before the stress of caregiving exceeds our human capacity to provide care. This stress affects your marriage, relationships with your friends and children, your career, and, in many cases, your sanity. As your life falls apart from caregiving, the quality of the care you can provide for your loved one will get decrease, but because of the stress, you won't even know it.

If you are not careful, caregiving can kill you. If you compare rates of depression, chronic illness, and early death between caregivers and non-caregivers, you will find that the caregivers get the short end of that stick. In addition, because of the caregiving burden, caregivers frequently reduce their work hours or make other changes to their work schedules that can put their jobs and income in jeopardy. Many caregivers may retire early or use their own money to support their loved one that endangers or even bankrupts their own retirement and future.

In our love story, they family greatly reduced caregiving stress by placing Laura in a nursing home and getting a full time caregiver for Mike at home. His children only needed to make sure that the nursing home was providing good care for Laura and that Mike's caregiver was doing a good job. They didn't have the stress of 24-hour care for both parents. For mom, the nursing home provided activities for Laura's active body, made sure she was clean, got dressed in the morning, and ate. For dad, the outside caregiver helped Mike with toileting, eating, and dressing, moving from his bed to a wheel chair, etc. Mike's children, Jason and his two sisters were able to advocate for dad's care without the stress of caregiving affecting their marriages, careers, friendships, and child raising. Yet, even with someone outside of the family providing this care, they were able to stay close and be there at the end. Because they did some advanced planning, Medicaid paid for Laura's nursing home care and Mike's savings for his private care, leaving the children with enough energy to support themselves and make sure their parents received the best care possible.

However, there might not be Medicaid available to pay for nursing home care, you may not have the money to pay for private in-home care, or you'll have the desire to provide that care yourself. In these situations, a very dedicated family member tries to provide the best care possible. As the demands and rigors of the care increase, family caregivers become sleep deprived and do not rest as much as they should. This can cause car accidents and medication errors. Each of these can have disastrous consequences. In fact, one third of all hospital admissions in the elderly are caused by medication errors. Rest is important, so give yourself some rest.

In many situations, the caregiver becomes financially dependent on the elder. The son or daughter quits his or her job and moves in to take care of dad. They have no savings and no other way of making money, other than to live off what mom has. This can create its own dangers with future Medicaid eligibility at stake as well as potential elder abuse claims if things are not prepared correctly.

So, be aware of the need to rest and the dangers of caregiving to yourself. Hire caregivers, seek respite care, or let other family members, friends, or social agencies help you provide care. Arrange for people to watch your elder for at least a few hours, so you can take a break and do other things for both your elder and yourself. Many nursing or assisted living facilities will allow your loved one to stay temporarily, maybe a week at a time, allowing you to rest or take a vacation.

If you do it all, you will buckle and then feel guilty about having human limits. You need rest and time to work and enjoy your own life, spouse and children. This is the only that way will you be able to provide the best care.

Guiding Principle Four – Checklist

❑ Caring for yourself is the most important thing you can do for both you and your parent.

❑ Schedule days off. Schedule vacations.

❑ Use all the help that is available from outside sources: siblings, neighbors, friends, or anyone else who offers help.

❑ Decide how much you are able to give and when you need help.

❑ Accept your limits and curb your instinct to fix everything.

❑ Find out how to use your energies most effectively. See what you can do and what you have to stop trying to do.

❑ Find a support group (helps you realize your situation is not unique and that others have the same feelings).

❑ Pursue other interests and hobbies (helps clear your mind and regain your balance and energy).

❑ Monitor the quality of your sleep. If it's too low, get help.

❑ Protect important relationships in your life.

Honor Your Loved One and Preserve Their Independence as Long as Medically Advisable

Who really wants to go into a nursing home? No one. Even the really high-end assisted living facilities and nursing homes seem amazing from the outside, but most people still want to stay in their homes. This is what their dignity demands.

Sometimes placement outside the home is appropriate, and sometimes it's not. The general rule we apply is: if their mind is gone (at a point where they no longer know where they are) then they shouldn't be at home. If they don't know what's going on, they have a one-minute memory and high caregiving expenses, it might make more sense to put them in a facility that is full of experienced caregivers, health care providers, and systems that provide high quality, advanced care.

If one of your parents is caregiving for the other at home, or if you are caregiving for a spouse at home, you must pay close attention to the "healthy" spouse. This is another thing to consider when deciding whether or not to keep someone at home. Caregiver stress kills. If the "healthy" spouse compromises her health because of caregiving stress, there is a chance that they could die before the "unhealthy" spouse or even become disabled herself.

For this reason, if the caregiving stress is too high, you must place the other person in a facility outside the home.

If dad's dementia behavior wakes mom up every two hours at night for whatever reason, then mom's stress level will dramatically increase. This added stress, in addition to the lack of sleep, could rapidly decrease mom's health. This is the time to think about placement.

As long as it will be safe, keep your loved one at home or in a non-nursing home community setting. Also, consider independent or assisted living facilities, as well as community programs that can provide additional support.

One of the many barriers to staying home is finding the money to pay for the additional care your loved one will need to stay there. There are several options which include: using income from social security, pensions, or investments; using money from savings and investments, reverse mortgages, Medicare, Medicaid, and loans from family members.

The magic formula to make someone's money last forever is to pay living and care expenses out of income without touching principal. For those who are have these resources, pensions and social security income may pay your loved one's entire monthly living expenses. For others, there may be only social security income, which is often not enough. As a result, generating more income is the first step in paying for care.

For example, for a person who holds most of her assets in deposit accounts, certificates of deposit, or other low interest bearing accounts, investing these assets more aggressively may create enough additional monthly income to make up any shortfall in income versus expenses.

If you want to keep your loved one in his or her home, but need additional funds to pay for caregivers, you could look into reverse mortgages (including private family mortgages). Since they are so expensive, we recommend reverse mortgages only if there are no other sources of money, including family. To do this, you must make sure that you have a financial plan. We talk about this in detail in Guiding Principle Six.

In our love story, Mike and Jason did all they could to give Laura her independence. But because Laura's Alzheimer's disease induced hallucinations and created other care needs, the stress became too much, and Mike could no longer care for her at home. As a result, Jason and Mike had no choice other than to put Laura in a nursing home. On the other hand, as Mike's disease progressed, he was able to stay at home with a caregiver and without his children's direct assistance. He was able to tell the caregiver what he wanted and when and did not have to rely on his children for that help. Mike was able to have independent care from his family, not be a burden to them, and maintain the highest level of dignity at the end of his life.

Guiding Principle Five – Checklist

❑ Determine whether it is safe for your loved one to stay at home.

❑ Set short and long-term housing goals (stay at home, live with relative, retirement residences, independent or assisted living, group home, skilled nursing facility).

❑ Look at your caregiver support network. Are caregivers (including the "healthy" spouse) endangering themselves by the stress caused by caregiving?

❑ Have you maximized your loved one's income and investments to provide money to pay for caregiving and living expenses?

❑ Investigate loans and funds available beyond investments so your love one can stay at home.

❑ Determine what in-home assistance will be needed (homemakers, home health care, grooming, etc.)

❑ If staying at home, get a professional (such as a care manager) to review home hazards and help remove or minimize them.

❑ Make sure your loved one is a safe driver/monitor their ability to drive.

❑ Find other transportation options (family, friends, rideshare, car pools, public transportation, senior housing with transportation services).

❑ Minimize social isolation and inactivity.

Guiding Principle Six
Make a Financial Plan

Providing for caregivers in the home, and paying for assisted living or for long-term care in a nursing home can be quite expensive. You will need to take steps to ensure that your loved one's money lasts as long as possible. The longer his or her funds last, the more care options there are, and the more independence and choices your loved one can still have.

Encourage your loved one to create a financial plan (including long-term care insurance, if possible) that will generate enough income to pay for long-term care at home, in an assisted living facility, or in a nursing home when finally needed. Don't wait until it's too late.

While planning, you should keep in mind the benefits somebody can obtain from using resources from Medicare, Veterans Administration benefits, and Medicaid. Without this, your loved one may be spending much more money on care than if he or she planned ahead.

The first step is to create an income stream large enough to pay for care without needing to dip into your assets each month. For many, this is difficult to do. The best professional to help with this is your financial planner. He or she will be able to help you structure the assets so that they can produce the maximum level of income while minimizing investment risk as much as possible.

If your loved one's income or long-term care insurance will not be able to pay for all of the long-term care expenses, encourage your loved one to consider an estate plan that includes Medicare, Veterans Administration, and Medicaid planning. A well-crafted estate and financial plan will give you the flexibility you will want when your loved one can no longer live alone and without help. This plan should accommodate any special family dynamics (such as special needs family members, potential conflicts between adult children, second marriages, and more). In addition, if there is no plan in place, or you think it is too late to plan, there are still things you can do.

In our love story, Jason brought his father to an elder law attorney to get help with Mike and Laura's care. Through proper Medicaid planning, Mike was able to put Laura into a nursing home with state and federal funds paying for most of her care. Mike also worked with a financial planner to make sure he could live off income saved through the Medicaid planning. Several years later when Mike developed ALS, he used the income from the financial plan to pay for his full-time caregiver. His Social Security benefits and investment income did not completely cover his caregiver costs, but he was able to plan enough to outlast his money and stay at home.

Sometimes, when funds are short, the last option is for the adult children to financially support the parent. If you do this, there are several issues to consider. The first issue is how the Medicaid eligibility rules treat gifts between family members. The second issue is how you can protect your parents' dignity as you support them.

Medicaid considers services between family members, or money given to family members, a gift. So, unless you take certain precautions, any amount of money that you give to your parents to help them buy food, pay household expenses, or pay medical bills is technically a gift from you to your parents. If your parent later goes into a nursing home or assisted living facility and sells their home, they will need to use the proceeds from the sale to pay for their nursing home or assisted living stay. Many times, the parent wants to repay her adult child for the gifts of support before using all of her money to pay for care (then the adult child could use that money again to support their parent, if needed). Of course, once your parent uses all of those funds to pay for care, she will need Medicaid benefits to do so. Under Medicaid's eligibility rules, you won't be penalized for giving a gift to your parent. However, a gift from the parent to the child is penalized. In fact, Medicaid will penalize any gift from the parent to the child (or anyone else) made within five years of seeking Medicaid benefits.

This means you should structure any money you give to your parent as a loan instead of a gift. Medicaid's rules do not penalize loan repayments, only gifts. The most effective way to prove there was a loan instead of a gift is with a written and signed promissory note. So, any money that a child gives to a parent should be accompanied by a written loan document or promissory note. If there is a written loan document between child and parent, Medicaid's eligibility rules will no longer penalize repayment of the "gifts"/"loan" after mom sells the house. That way, prior to applying for Medicaid, mom can pay back to her child the money the child lent her without accepting charity (and by doing that, maintain her dignity and financial independence).

Not only do Medicaid rules classify transfers of money between family members as gifts subject to penalties, but those rules also consider a child's physical caregiving and support assistance for her parent to be an uncompensated gift of services. If your parent later pays you for doing these things, Medicaid will penalize him or her for giving you a "gift," As you need to make a written loan agreement to repay loans after the house sells, you should also create a written "personal care agreement" that documents the parent will be paying her child for providing care (whether or not the child accepts the money). So, if an adult child provides caregiving support for a parent, consider a written caregiving agreement (*in advance of providing services – this cannot be done retroactively*) with a reasonable hourly rate since Medicaid will not permit the parent to pay the child otherwise. If this arrangement is not in writing, authorities might not honor them, as many state laws say that all services and money from close family members are gifts unless you can prove otherwise in writing. Remember, Medicaid penalizes gifts made within five years of seeking benefits.

The second issue is protecting your parents' dignity. Many are reluctant to accept help from children because they believe they should be able to support themselves. This is part of their concept of independence and self-reliance. Nobody wants to rely on somebody else for help. By entering into a written loan agreement to eventually repay any funds that a child gives to their parent, the parent knows that she will eventually pay her child back if there's anything left before Medicaid makes her spend it all on her care.

Guiding Principle Six - Checklist

❑ Estimate elder care-related expenses (in the home alone, with help in the home, in a setting outside the home.

❑ Investigate long-term care insurance options.

❑ Maximize income from investment assets.

❑ Find other resources or income to pay for living expenses and care.

   ✓ Medicare, Medicaid and Veteran's Benefits

   ✓ Pensions and Social Security

   ✓ Reverse mortgage or home equity loan

   ✓ Loans from children, relatives or insurance policies

❑ Watch what you give your loved one so that support does not affect their eligibility for other benefits, such as Medicaid (make the support you give a loan, not a gift – loans must be in writing and signed)

❑ If your loved one will be paying you to provide caregiving services, you must have a written contract between you and your loved one that specifies the tasks you do and your hourly rate of pay. You must also keep timesheets to document when and how you provided those services.

❑ Consider family dynamics (personality issues, special needs beneficiaries) when determining who has access to money, financial records, etc.

Guiding Principle Seven
Respect Your Loved One's End-of-Life Wishes

As the last chapter of somebody's life begins to close, many times the person only has their family and personal dignity left. It's your job as the caregiver to do all you can to honor that dignity, as well as the wishes that preserve it. Remember, you want to add life to their years, not simply years to their life.

There will come a time when your loved one cannot tell you what he or she wants. Take the time now to discuss your loved one's feelings on life-sustaining medical treatment and hospice, last rites, and final resting place. Let the rest of the family unit know these feelings so that you can honor those wishes without strife when the time comes.

The decision on whether or not to remove life-sustaining treatment can be a very sensitive issue. Some people want every medical procedure that can be done to keep them alive. There are other people who just want to go quietly, with enough pain medications to rest in peace. It's essential you understand what your loved one wants. Death, in itself, is not failure. Some families think they have failed if they have not used every medical procedure and technology available to extend life. However, this life extension often comes with more difficult problems (bedsores, infections, worse illnesses, etc.) that cause great suffering. Your loved one will die nonetheless.

Some of the most traumatic situations occur when the spouse or adult children do not understand the dying person's wishes. Each is trying to maintain what they think dignity demands, and many times that creates a situation where families fight and family harmony is lost. The second level of trauma can occur right after death, at the burial. Make sure that your loved one arranges a prepaid funeral to avoid issues at the funeral home.

Letting your loved one die with dignity is important. Dying with dignity means making sure that you help carry out the dying person's last wishes. For example, many people do not want to be on life support for an extended period of time or do not want to be kept alive "with all of those tubes coming out of [them]." You don't want someone who won't be able to "let go" at the end be your loved one's health care decision maker. No one wants to die slowly and in pain. If there is one child who cannot let go of mom at the end, for their own reasons, then don't let that child be the ultimate decision maker under a health care power of attorney because they will not honor mom's last wishes. You have to have the right person doing this.

In our love story, the most important thing for Mike was to stay at home and be with his wife, Laura. Despite the ravages of his disease, he still knew where he was and what was happening to him. Through the 24-hour caregiver and support of his family, he did what most of us would like to do—stay and die at home. In fact, by asking his children to bring Laura back from the nursing home for a visit, he was able to be with her at the end surrounded by family.

Guiding Principle Seven - Checklist

❑ Death is not failure. Will the next medical procedure cause additional pain and needless suffering?

❑ Find out from your loved one what his or her wishes are for end-of-life care:

  ✓ Level of medical intervention (does she want aggressive medical treatment?)

  ✓ Pain management

  ✓ Dying at home

  ✓ Comfort Care

  ✓ Hospice

❑ Determine how much family harmony your loved one wants you to protect.

❑ Share information with other family members to keep conflict and suspicion low.

❑ Watch your own activity for burnout. Get help early. Take breaks.

❑ Embrace hospice care and the hospice care team of doctors, nurses, aides, social workers, clergy, and volunteers.

❑ Have family members exchange heartfelt words and offer acts of forgiveness.

❑ Be aware of your loved one's goals and milestones:

    ✓ Last wishes

    ✓ Family events

    ✓ Important projects to complete

    ✓ Personal goals

❑ Spend quality time with your loved one. Your presence alone is valuable to him or her.

❑ Plan funeral arrangements, memorial services, and post-death legal matters.

Guiding Principle Eight
You Can't Control a Progressive Disease or Sudden Illness

There are some health conditions that improve and respond to treatment. There are some conditions that do not, no matter what you do. Understand the condition or ailment that your loved one has, and do not expect miracles to happen. Manage from that point forward. People don't recover from dementia, Alzheimer's disease, or major strokes often.

At life's end, the decision on whether or not to perform more medical procedures to keep a person alive longer is a difficult one. Many times, extra treatments do not necessarily extend life, but cause pain and have many side effects that can create needless suffering.

Here are two examples:

1. There was a *New York Times* article written on an expert pancreatic doctor who closed up his practice after he was diagnosed with cancer. He lived his life with his children and only took pain meds. He just accepted his fate and lived his life with grace.

2. Dartmouth Medical School released a study in 2008 that compared end-of-life care between UCLA medical Center and the Mayo Clinic. The cost of the end-of-life care decisions and number of procedures ordered at UCLA was double that at the Mayo Clinic.

The study concluded that the additional end-of-life care procedures ordered at UCLA did not necessarily improve people's end-of-life care. In fact, the Mayo Clinic kept people in the hospital 35% fewer days than at UCLA. Wouldn't you like to spend 35% less of your last days in the hospital?

We recommend you continue treating your loved one's diseases, but keep in mind their dignity and end-of-life wishes when you decide on how much medical care they need at the end of their life. Sometimes, less is more.

In our love story, Mike and his family realized the limitations of the degenerative diseases that both he and Laura had. For Laura, her Alzheimer's disease symptoms were irreversible. Her mind was gone—she couldn't recognize or remember anyone—but her body was strong and healthy. The family couldn't control anything other than to put her in a place where she would get the care she needed. For Mike it was more difficult. His disease affected the nerve cells, which activated his voluntary muscle movement. In a sense, his mind became trapped in a failing body. Unfortunately, there was no treatment that would cure his disease. After a while, Mike accepted his fate and so did his family. They did not opt for expensive and aggressive medical treatments; they accepted what was happening and made it through the best they could.

Guiding Principle Eight - Checklist

❑ Research the disease. Get accurate information on its progression so you and your loved one can participate actively in care and make informed decisions.

❑ Maintain your loved one's dignity during the process. Find out their practical goals in treatment, rehabilitation, pain management, and independence.

❑ Determine if changes in your loved one's environment/equipment will improve your loved one's quality of life (for example, a wheeled walking frame may dramatically improve mobility).

❑ Learn the things you can and cannot control. Focus on what you can control. Let go of the things you cannot control.

❑ Try to mindfully enjoy the moment.

❑ Add life to years, not years to life. Think carefully about how much pain and suffering additional aggressive medical procedures will cause.

Guiding Principle Nine
A Nursing Home Placement Isn't a Death Sentence

No one wants to go to a nursing home. Thirty or 40 years ago, families remember taking care of their loved one at home until they died. Back then, people typically didn't last more than several months, but with the advances in medicine, people who are sick now live much longer. Families need to rethink their objections to nursing homes as they increase our end-of-life lifespans.

Also, nursing homes are not what they were 30 or even 20 years ago. Modern skilled nursing care, if done correctly, can meet the high demand medical and care needs of a severely disabled person. It can also help keep him as safe and as healthy as his condition permits. The trained staff at these facilities can, many times, perform better caregiving then a family member or a caregiver can do at home.

Providing skilled care in a nursing home is very difficult. Although facilities are much better than they used to be, constant vigilance, unannounced visits, and guiding of care will still be necessary make sure your loved one receives the best care. While there are many facilities that are good, there are still many that may not provide good care.

Many times, nursing home placement is appropriate because the care will be better. However, it's important to research the facility before you put your loved one in it. The website at medicare.gov has a function to search for the quality of your loved one's potential nursing home. Pick the places that have high ratings and watch them closely.

In our love story, Mike found a nursing home for Laura to stay in. It was not the fanciest place; in fact, it looked kind of drab. But the staff was bright and cheerful, listened to Mike and his children about the special things that Laura was still able to enjoy, and provided good care that matched Laura's needs. Placement for Laura lifted a heavy burden off the family, enabling them to transition from being the primary caregivers for Laura to her best advocate for high quality care. Things would have been much worse if they did not make the decision to place Laura in a nursing home.

Guiding Principle Nine - Checklist

Deciding to make the move

❏ Have a doctor or Geriatric Care Manager conduct a Geriatric Assessment to assess your loved one's physical and mental status, especially to perform primary and secondary activities of daily living.

❏ Can your loved one stay safely at home with some additional, outside help?

❏ Can you loved one afford to pay this help or are there community resources to provide this help? (Look at the U.S. Administration on Aging's Elder Care Locator http://www.eldercare.gov/Eldercare.NET/Public/Index.aspx)

❏ Does your loved one still have the mental capacity to realize where she is?

Choosing a nursing home

❏ Pick a facility with high ratings. (medicare.gov/NursingHomeCompare/search.aspx)

❏ How close is that facility to your home/work? (the closer, the better)

❏ Is the facility certified under the Medicare program?

❏ Is the facility certified under the Medicaid program?

❑ Does the facility provide both skilled care and custodial care? (Skilled care is for a short time after hospitalization. Custodial care is for a longer period of time. Check if your loved one will need to move rooms if she goes from one level of care to another)

❑ Does the nursing home have a state license?

❑ Do they do criminal background checks on the workers and residents?

❑ Is there a high ratio of nurses and nurse's aides to residents?

❑ Evaluate Quality of Life, Quality of Care, Nutrition and Hydration, and Safety with Medicare's Checklist. (www.medicare.gov/nursing/checklist.asp)

Guiding Principle Ten
Try to Mitigate Family Conflict

Family conflict at the end of a parent's life is sometimes inevitable. However, typically the greatest asset for any person is for their children to get along after they die. If you have the chance to plan ahead or even react on-the-fly, knowing the triggers of family conflict can help you decide whether you can avoid conflict or whether it is inevitable.

The five most common triggers of family conflict are:

✓ Arguments over distribution of money and assets after death, including homes, antiques, keepsakes

✓ Rifts in the family that caregiver stress causes

✓ Dysfunctional relationships between siblings and parent and child and old hurts which have not yet healed

✓ Siblings and parents who live in different parts of the country and who do not communicate frequently enough

✓ Sibling wealth disparity

Despite dysfunctional families, many times there are ways to prevent the conflict from exploding. A third party is sometimes needed to make decisions. Sometimes, just transparency and disclosure will help.

Other times, with a little more help and understanding, the children can make it through and help their parents maintain their dignity as well as family harmony.

Family conflict at the end of a parent's life is often a result of old sibling rivalries, geographical distances, and sibling wealth disparities. Know these issues may exist and, if appropriate, include siblings in the decision making process; communication and transparency is key to loving one another at the end while helping your parent.

If you know there's going to be a family fight over something then give it away in advance. Watch out for the sibling conflict in particular. The first question I ask when new clients come in is, "How well do your children get along?" This relationship makes all the difference in the world.

In our love story, we did not have family conflict. Some situations are like this, where all the family members agree and get along. Generally, when the parties share information with each other about the elder who isn't well, are able to weigh in on major decisions, and have physical access to the elder, there are no problems or suspicions. However, sometimes conflict is inevitable and you cannot avoid it no matter what you do.

Guiding Principle Ten - Checklist

❑ Many conflicts are based on suspicion of bad actions and lack of trust. In some instances, sharing information freely, providing access to mom and/or dad, and making decisions collaboratively will ease or eliminate conflict.

❑ For each adult sibling, identify what goal he or she wants to achieve, what information is needed, and who will research it.

❑ Actively listen to the other person's point of view. People cannot listen to someone else's point of view until they feel someone has listened to their own point of view first.

❑ Is there a family member who has a severe personality defect or mental illness?

❑ During active listening, identify a person's interests in the conflict and ask yourself why they have those interests. Interests may include: needs, wishes, values, aspirations, fears, and concerns. Make a point of checking in with the other person to make sure that you understand their point and that they feel both heard and understood. Understanding the why can be the basis of finding a solution.

❑ Separate a person's interests from their positions on issues. Think of positions as their "conclusions" on an issue which may include: their opinions, their solution, their "non-negotiables," etc.

- ❑ After you identify issues and positions, determine viable options through brainstorming options, considering those options, and evaluating them in detail.

- ❑ Include mom or dad's voice and wishes in the decisions.

- ❑ If things get rough, get mediation.

- ❑ Get attorneys involved. Generally, they are levelheaded and scream at each other less than fighting family members do.

Professional Responsibility and Rewards

Guiding clients through complicated and emotional legal situations requires more than the usual consulting skills. You'll face old sibling rivalries, geographical distances, and wealth disparities, among other challenges specific to this practice area. Knowing these issues may exist and how to address them is key to maintaining transparency while helping your client.

The first question we ask when new clients come in is, "How well do your family members get along?" These relationships make all the difference in the world, and your kindness, knowledge and skills as a trusted counselor and legal advisor is what will keep those clients and their families satisfied with your services and coming back for more.

Resources & Endnotes

"The Complete Eldercare Planner" by Joy LoVerde

"Mom Always Liked You Best: A Guide for Resolving Family Feuds, Inheritance Battles, & Eldercare Crises" by Arline Kardasis, Rikk Larsen, Crystal Thorp, Blair Trippe

"How to Care for Aging Parents" by Virginia Morris

"Creating Moments of Joy" by Jolene Brackey

"A Bittersweet Season: Caring for Our Aging Parents and Ourselves" by Jane Gross

"The 36-Hour Day" by Nancy L. Mace and Peter V. Rabins

"To Survive Caregiving" by Cheryl E. Woodson

Schulz, R. & Beach, S. (1999). Caregiving as a risk factor for mortality: The Caregiver Health Effects Study, *JAMA*, 282: 2215-2219.

About the author

Ben Neiburger is an active member of the National Academy of Elder Law Attorneys (NAELA) and a member of the Executive Committee and Board of Directors for the Illinois Institute of Continuing Legal Education. Through frequent speaking engagements and ongoing course work both locally and nationally, Ben is in continuous pursuit of knowledge and insight to the laws and finances that affect our families and senior citizens. He brings this wealth of knowledge, his clear and common sense explanations, his patience, gentle humor and sensitivity to each of his legal consultations.

In addition to being admitted to the Bar of the United States Supreme Court, Mr. Neiburger is a member of the National Academy of Elder Law Attorneys, the National Speakers Association, DuPage County Estate Planning Council, Illinois State Bar Association, and Elmhurst Chamber of Commerce.

Ben lives in Oak Park, Illinois with his wife, two teenaged sons and a menagerie of pets.

Reach the author

Ben Neiburger, JD, CPA
GENERATION LAW, LTD
747 N. Church Rd., Suite B4B
Elmhurst IL 60126
630-782-1766
Ben@GenerationLaw.com

Ask Ben about speaking at your next professional association meeting!

Available Now!

"Brighter Skies"

The consumer version of this helpful guide, with the same common sense language and handy checklists.

Legal and financial professionals are invited to purchase "Brighter Skies" in bulk to give to your clients as a valuable take-away. We encourage you to place a label with your firm's name and contact information inside the cover, provide a custom bookmark, or attach a personalized highlighter pen. Your clients will know who to call and how to reach you when they're ready for the next step.

To Order

Call: 630-782-1766

Email: Books@GenerationLaw.com

Mail:

"Brighter Skies" Professional Quantity Discount

Retail at Amazon: $9.95 each
Direct through Generation Law:
    1-10 copies @ $8 each + $5 shipping
    11-25 copies @ $7 each + $10 shipping
    26-100 copies @ $6 each + free shipping

Qty _____ x $_____ each + shipping = $_____

Ship to: _____

Address: _____

City _____ **ST** _____ **ZIP** _____

Email _____

Please make check payable to Generation Law and mail with this form to: Generation Law, 747 N. Church Rd., Suite B4, Elmhurst IL 60126

www.ingramcontent.com/pod-product-compliance
Lightning Source LLC
Chambersburg PA
CBHW070402290526
45790CB00004B/1596